for Antonio,
Enjoy! :)

BUBBLY
By The Sea

B. K. Sweeting

Bubbly By The Sea

Learn more at www.Bksweeting.com

This is a work of creative non-fiction.
Some parts have been fictionalized in varying degrees, for various purposes.

First paperback edition—2020

Paperback ISBN: 978-1-09833-429-1
ebook ISBN: 978-1-09833-430-7

This book is lovingly dedicated,

to both my mom and little brother,

Robert.

Contents

PART ONE
HEAD

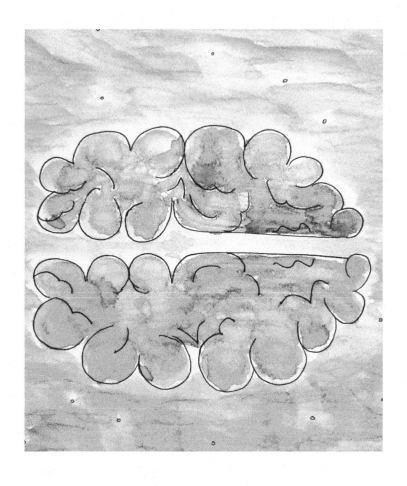

Feverish.
Temple to temple, dripping liquid gold.

Wipe your tears of fear,
Suspire.

Your mind, a complex algorithm.
Your heart, anatomical fortune.

Falling up, but you have never leapt.
I am here for you and have never left.

Jumping together,
We land in cosmopolitan.

Dream Factory

Stained glass,
And overhead lighting.
Scent of turned pages,
Almond and camphor.
A desired silence.
Sharing quick glances.
Refectory tables,
And mated seating.
Bountiful shelves.
With organized dividers.
Tall ladders on wheels,
Lead to vaulted ceilings.
Metal railings,
Meet maple and mahogany.

B. K. Sweeting

Autumn Action

Thick rimmed glasses and a warm jacket.
Apple cider donuts and cinnamon coffee.
An Autumnal way, to start the day.

Taking a stroll on leaf covered sidewalks.
String lights hang from cast iron posts.
Pumpkins on every corner, of this cape town border.

This time of year, seduces many souls.
Especially mine, as I make my way.
To return a mail-in ballot and demand change.

Sweet Chroma

Toffee, truffle, chocolate tart.
Intoxicating culture, radiant hearts.

Mocha, caramel, toasted beige.
I see you, in so many lovely shades.

You paint this world whole, in so many ways.
Your life matters – today, tomorrow and yesterday.

B. K. Sweeting

Beach Toast

Half past 2p, caramelized locks and bronzed skin.
A teal towel tucked in a soft bed of beige.
Lying on her belly, with a blank canvas.
Ceaseless sun kisses painted by sun rays.
Late in afternoon, on the California Coast.
No brunch cut offs, for delicious beach toast.

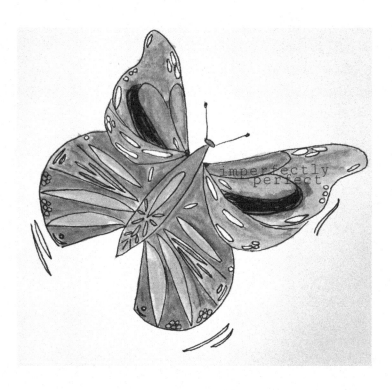

Butterfly

Floating somewhere, in the between.
It was they or them, no he or she.

Represented in every color.
An array of contrast, like no other.

Unique, but flying just as high.
As all the other girls and guys.

Soaring easy amongst the trees.
Amongst the lavender and Shasta daisies.

Extraordinary on the eyes.
But greater charm resides inside.
A butterfly.

B. K. Sweeting

#

In place.
Grab the snacks, stuff your face.

Black mirror in hand,
Post as much as we can.

Walk as far as the eye can see,
Approximately, twelve hundred square feet.

Never missing the tik tok,
But tick tock…

The hand on the clock.
Is moving, but ours is not.

It is time, our virtual ride arrives.
Where are we going, how will we rise?

Bubbly by the Sea

To have or not to have, routine.
Monday mimosa and charcuterie.
Green choices and staying clean.
Making the most of twenty twenty.

Feature movies in, virtually connect.
Tie dye sweats and wipes to disinfect.
Solo by the sea with bottomless bubbly.
In isolation, why not make it lovely?

Hike into sunset, weeks are fleeting.
Ten second commute, for a video meeting.
Planter box veggies and homemade baking.
Petition and walk, history in the making.

B. K. Sweeting

Ageless Lilies

Afternoon naps, swimming in a lake of reverie.
We pop our heads up, between oversized lilies.
Edge of water, we approach a meadow.
Prancing and dancing, to a tall weeping willow.
Swinging weightlessly from long tree leaves.
We laugh so hard; it pierces our bellies.
Smelling bushels of berries, freshly picked.
A mouthwatering thirst, that stirred and kicked.
Tasty end of Summer, delighting as we please.
Surrounded by the glimmer, as we catch some z's.

B. K. Sweeting

Frenemy Status

Gravity is a straight down frenemy.
She can slam us to the ground, and provide no empathy.
She will also keep us grounded, when we truly need.
The best friend, who will always be there,
Who will also have us trippin', on thin air.

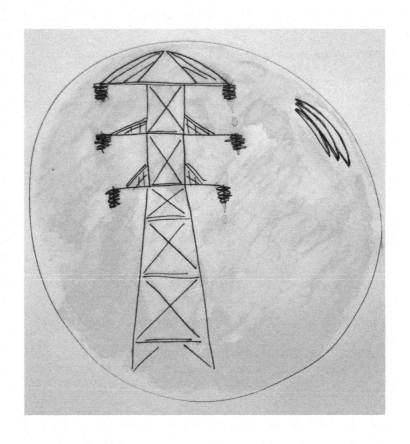

Filament

You are watching me,
I am watching him,
He is watching her,
And she is watching us.

Invisible thread marries knots and holes.
Delicately sewn, straight through our souls.
Electrical wires connecting us all.
Yet, we are not connected.
Not at all.

B. K. Sweeting

Clutch

Living in a digital world…
An opinionated score, of anger and bore.
Fake tunes, a symphony.
I reach for you; you reach for me.
No pastures, no swaying trees.
Plentiful cords, beneath the concrete.
All control and not for free.
We yearn to learn, to feel, to see.
We hold on tight; we are clutching.
On to something, but never touching.

Crescent

Typical lives, insistent on routine.
Cloudless skies, striving for pristine.
Scrambled minds, not always seen.
Abundant behaviors, craving relief.

So many scales on a spectrum.
Puzzling conditions, misrepresented.
Try to solve and put them all together.
Why spend time, to correct unseen weather?

How about a sliver of waxing phase.
Showcase support in an intriguing way.
A vibrant crescent, unisex gold.
Illumination and intention, growing so.

Acknowledging history, no need to cure.
Nothing to correct or force to be pure.
Neurotypical skies, are not the only to embark.
For stars shine brightest, viewed in the dark.

B. K. Sweeting

Boxes

Inconvenient, sheltering in place.
Wood beams and steel frame.
No where to go but a kitchen, pantry full.
A bathroom, with a basic toilet.
A living room to watch the same movies in.
A bed to sleep in, intermittently.
Tiresome, really.

Worn down, staying in place.
Solid stone under a highway.
Everywhere to go but home.
A kitchen at the end of a drive thru.
Your bathroom, city shrubbery.
Cardboard to sleep on, hard and freezing.
Wearisome, really.

Boxes, in so many shapes and sizes.
Some hold jewelry, some hold bodies.
Broken down in one domain, to recycle.
And become another's sanctuary.
Sleep soundly, but the knock on our box.
Has been patiently awaiting, a changing shock.

B. K. Sweeting

100 Million

Living on rez but we still exist.
Weren't we here first? History tries to override this.

Statues of you, over our sacred land.
Broken hearts and empty hands.

We have brains, we have heart.
Have the tools, to make beautiful art.

We play, we pray and work hard.
No running water, all under the stars.

Impoverished and owed.
Must we beg, must we plead?

For poverty you see,
It never truly sleeps.

Have you forgotten; we still bleed?
We still bleed…

B. K. Sweeting

Casting Call

The poor inspire the rich, the rich inspire the poor.
Exchanging rights, at a rate of 'either or'.

We hope and pray, to have what they have.
They go incognito, be as average as they can.

They say, "I wish I had the simple life,
Go out, where no one knows my name."

We say, "How much is this?"
Bills or dine out, we contemplate.

Sad stories, groundbreaking roles for them.
Award-winning speeches, our dated inspiration.

Mysteries unveiled, in turn helps the best of us.
Dusting them off, in desperation of justice.

All it takes, is the right casting call.
Bring darkness to light, make change for us all.

B. K. Sweeting

Vine, Conquisté

A luscious Hawaiian lei,
Around neck, over dark long waves.

She was a second generation,
But the first to graduation.

So proudly she stood, curvy and tall.
Onlooking mamá, confident she would never fall.

The courage it takes,
When so much is at stake.

You challenged her place,
But she worked hard, intellectual pace.

Books hold power, they change lives.
They change humanity, in the blink of an eye.

It is crucial for you to realize,
We all deserve a chance, for this world to thrive.

B. K. Sweeting

N 38° 20.448
W 123° 03.126

He resided with his family, along a coastal dune.
So far from home, a young life taken too soon.

An Italian adventure collided with murderers.
A mistaken car sought for valuable treasures.

The beauty in tragedy, lies within organ donation.
Over five lives, gained from giving salvation.

Sweet boy, they lost you in September.
The bells ring for you, we will always remember.

Old Vine

So many fine things, that wine brings.
Weddings, laughter, confidence to sing.

Mustard grass, lines up a field of dreams.
Out of towners, collect grape leaves.

Unfortunately, these vines, witnessed a tragic scene.
Untouched, until the fire of twenty seventeen.

Late in the night, of early October.
Flames claimed a county, in starless somber.

Lives, animals and homes, not overseen.
Panic from bed, brought on so painfully.

Resilient, rebuild and revive over time.
But they will never forget, the twenty-two lives.

B. K. Sweeting

Wildfire

Lightning strikes and not long until,
Blazes dance, across the hill.

An evacuation is our seasonal event.
Abandoning 700k homes, we own and rent.

Falling ash from the sky above.
Attempts to filter, as much as we could.

Thick smoke, chemicals and contaminant.
Air quality deadly, water tastes of laminate.

I do not remember, signing up for this.
I guess the fine print, my ancestors missed.

Bowing down my head in care,
For those, who have lost their lives here.

At what cost do we pay,
For a coastal sunset, at the end of the day?

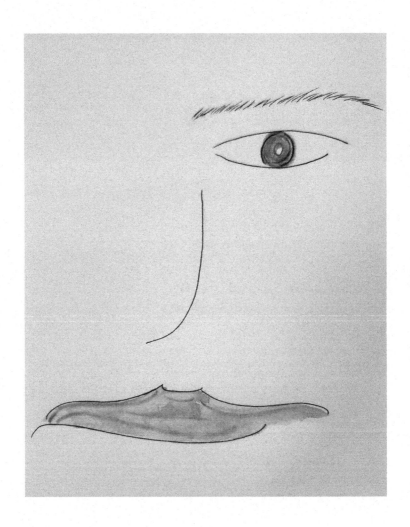

Anonymous

They had a name, that went without credit.
Women of every color lived through alias epoch.
In every way, shape and form.
Creating their present to future, free of thorn.
A garden of roses bound to intellect and beauty.
Behind closed terrace, fulfilling a duty.
Blooming flowers birth the next gen of daughters.
Would soon advise us, of the true-life authors.

B. K. Sweeting

100 Years

Little Girl…

Olive skinned, frizzy brunette.
A focus on pretty, pink barrettes.

Kitchen toys, kittens and play makeup.
Defined roles, we do not dare admit it.

Cute boys and poppy music.
'Are we still friends?' And retro lockets.

Climb a tree, but do not scuff your flats.
Adoring ponies, but never bats.

A vote is a vote, but a seat is not guaranteed.
Pay sacrificed and demand with no heed.

A hundred years has passed.
What has changed, a curious laugh.

Gazing into her eyes I ask,
"What do you want? Now go be that."

Tug of War

We must be everything.
Office, nurse babies to "what can I bring?"

Questioning ourselves, endlessly.
Not showing pain, conspicuously.

Our body, our rights.
Wait, this is ours, right?

They say 'Tug of War' is child's play.
No sir, that is our day to day.

Emotion, but do not get carried away.
It is still their world and their way.

So, excuse me miss, what do you say?
The time is now, it was yesterday.

B. K. Sweeting

Trust Her

"I see your tears, I understand fuss.
But infinite stardust, lives within us.

Aesthetic and looks, come and go.
Refinement and grace are the best of those.

The thing in your chest, the thing in your head.
Invest in those, put your doubts to bed.

You've a gleaming future ahead.
Cheer up miss.", my mother always said.

Home

Stainless-steel straws.
Ban single-use plastic.
Why isn't it working faster?
Silly human, impatience is classic.

Our mistake to Mother Nature…
We owed her much more.
Bringing change only,
Under wrath of her scorn.

Temperatures rising,
Rain, rain, went away.
Does it have to end this way?
Could we nurture her and stay?

Creature of habit.
But if your habits do not change,
A calm to crisis, will be what you crave.
For your home could then, reside under waves.

B. K. Sweeting

Beauty and the Bees

Never restricted to allure.
A dazzling creature, lively book warm.
Flowing dress, in her favorite yellow.
Blending well, in a field of daffodils.
This damsel did not need a savior.
She was a savior.
Warrior for the environment.
Queen bee for the fallen.
Planting, marching and signing petitions.
Knowing no borders, for sake of a future.
A tale best read in sunshine.

Clovers

I Irish danced, as a young girl.
Most freeing, yet structured dance in the world.

Toes tapping, leaps and keeping pace.
Thumbs down, moving with speed and grace.

Favorite part was mom curling hair.
Feis dresses, sparked Celtic flair.

Dressing makeup, a light layer.
Magical memories, I will always bare.

Nana brought me to County Cork,
Heavenly scenes, from shore to shore.

Folk music and old castles galore.
Eye-popping greens, needing nothing more.

The women in my life, gave a cultural gift.
A clover treasure, everlasting bliss.

B. K. Sweeting

Nana

Countertop, full glass of red wine.
Bacon, broth and fresh cut thyme.

Garden carrots, onion and sage.
All memorized, no recipe page.

Crema over simmer, low and slow.
Chicken, mushroom and sweet potato.

Flavors wed, till tender do us part.
A one pot dish made from the heart.

Hardwood floors and native baskets.
Quaint décor and large red carpets.

Full bookshelves, of twice read novels.
Nana's essence, worthy of being bottled.

B. K. Sweeting

Thirty Candles

Going at life, thirty miles per hour.
Who knew she possessed such little power?
Tried to be strong, avoid the word weak.
How she endured this, every damn week.
Months went by, goals unchecked.
No creative income, no six figure checks.
Hungry artist with abundance to write.
Mountains of content lived inside her mind.
No true following and no buyers galore.
But a loving mother, to lift her off the floor.
She said, "Envision a best you,
Live her life to make it true."
She did as her mom said.
Looked the part, made her bed.
A passion for words, change and paint.
Focusing hard, in a cosmic state.
Flying ideas and shooting stars.
Birthed a sparkling and brand-new start.

Life Palette

She traveled through the forest of gray.
Desperate thoughts, on this gloomy day.

On Appaloosa horseback, she traveled away.
Changing color, was the price to pay.

Mood then ambition, with action to follow.
All she wanted, was to rid of the hollow.

Swiftly past branches and looming trees.
Craving meaningful life, not a digital tease.

Approaching edge of forest.
She chucked away her phone.

Adrenaline and determination,
To find a real home.

Drops of cadmium red lights.
Experiencing a passionate drive.

Flicker of hasa yellow brights.
A joyful and optimistic sight.

Splashes of cerulean blues,
Discovery, balance and calmness too.

Finally, a world, where feeling whole.
Would soon, accrue.

War on Oil

On the battlefield of critics,
Canvases collect dust.
A gallery of fools.
Who could one trust?
These hands, blood and bones.
Regain strength.
Back to incognito.

B. K. Sweeting

Art on the Go

Needles and immeasurable hours.
Pursuing our human superpowers.

An hourglass and vine of florals.
Crowned hearts, eclectic murals.

What does yours say about you?
A loved one's name, fifty stars on blue?

Passionately displayed.
History, stories, our cultural ways.

'What about when you age?', They say.
Adding, "You're going to regret that, someday."

Well by then, I hope your judgement subsides.
Hope you have lived and become wise.

For we will not be worrying about your eyes.
Instead, cherishing our once creative sides.

B. K. Sweeting

How are you?

Are you pretending to smile,
Gritting teeth, in your sleep,
Scream into your pillow,
Shower cry, not making a peep,
Holding your breath, sporadically?

I would like to ask one more thing,
Would you hold on for me?
Exhale and breathe in deep.
The storm will pass, with a rainbow to reap.

B. K. Sweeting

Next Episode

The last scenes may have been rough,
Running, to all lead up to this.

Grab the popcorn and get cozy,
This season of your life is about to get good.

B. K. Sweeting

See This

Take it as a sign.
To live that first-rate, kind of life.
Eat right, get sleep tonight.
Health is wealth, heal your mind.

B. K. Sweeting

Time

Every flow in a moment, is crucially valuable.
But know, there's always time to change direction.
Your path current is not set, it is malleable.

B. K. Sweeting

Just Be

B. K. Sweeting

Breathe

An uneven scale, of good and bad.
A long way to go, but do not go mad.
Condemning the finer things,
For the sake of unjust things.
Is to condemn happiness.
For the reality of sadness.
To be aware, educated and proactive.
To also eat, drink, play and be active.
No shame to prefer wine over water.
Be everything at once? Do not bother.
All is aligned, you are doing the best you can.
Take a breath and get a lay of the land.
Could be five, ten or fifteen years later.
Haven't you heard, 'better late than never.'
Make goals with that wild ambition.
Meanwhile, welfare first and then your mission.

B. K. Sweeting

Insight

One small decision away.

Make troubles seem like yesterdays.

A moment to turn off the tv,

Phone down, back stretching.

You always dreamt of,

Life in the city or off in the mountains.

No reason to not be there,

No obligation or fears.

A highest self.

Surrounded by wealth,

Could be friendship, or tall bookshelves.

Inventing, painting or curing cancer cells.

Design the hearts desire.

Never let passion retire.

Take insight,

And intentionally live,

Your dream life.

Clean

Supple skin, legs extend, in a hot bath.

These grapes in glass, no longer taste of the past.

Moving on from memories, a prized mental clarity.

Time for letting go and coming clean.

Letting the self-respect, wash over me.

PART TWO

HEART

B. K. Sweeting

Sunday Night

Clean sheets, warm bodies.
The way you play with my hair,
Tugging on my heart strings.
Our window ajar, the smell of rain.
All of it sends little shock waves,
Through my veins.

Imperial Eyes

Rising away from my bed, buoyant.
All that I knew, starts to fade.
Bright greens, tease from under a blanket of fog.
Delicate mist pricks the hair on my arms.
A welcomed stillness, presented.
Cheeks pink, from a beatific chill.
Symmetrical vine and tree, in axial halcyon.
Tender blue above, viridescent below.
Waterspouts in slow motion.
Gold sculptures crafted with devotion.
Balmy honey, mandarin and cardamom.
A nectar that dusts the edge of my nose.

Clink

Slowly unveiling my eyes, adjusting gaze.
Brought to eye level, a dainty cup atop a toile saucer.
"Tea dear?", his olive eyes inquiring.
Still wearing the smile from the garden,
I reply, "thank you my love."

Water and Wood

Lightfoot through wooded peace.
Nothing on, but the smile you gave me.

Feeling so small, beneath the redwood trees.
Mist to droplets, fall off fern leaves.

Skin damp, a sublime tease.
Face fresh, free from impurities.

You bring me down to my knees.
In the middle of no where, celestial and free.

You present this liberty to me,
To explore, to be…

To be loved by you,
While encouraging me to breathe.

Cashmere Daydreams

Together we explore,
Pastel waves on a starry floor.

Swirling soft pinks, in silky drinks.
Cotton candy sky and precious winks.

Half under a pergola of trust.
Natural light, sun pecking us.

Shimmer bubbles, floating in pool.
Hillside air keeps us feeling cool.

A place with opalescent trees,
With violin hums and piano keys.

These cashmere daydreams.
Just you, just me.

Milk on Mars

Holographic castle, blank tv screens.
Cut-out jeans and oversized white tees.

No future and no past.
I cling to you, through a fog of gas.

Pops of vibrant, lavender riots.
Iridescent lilacs, nothing quite like it.

Sifting through treasure, your shiny dime.
Your kiss tastes of key lime pie.

Twirling, whirling, all the while.
You win again, most amusing smile.

Somehow feeling weak in knees,
Even with, no gravity.

Not an otherworldly tease,
The chained life on earth, we happily leave.

B. K. Sweeting

Read Me

Wet morning, café cappuccino.
A puzzle less interesting, forces him to scan the room.

Noticing me across the way.
Enticed curiosity.

He abandons the comfort of his warm nook.
Large soles, creak hardwood below.

Running a finger down my spine,
Incites a feel, that cannot be defined.

He offers me a spot at his table.
Submissive, I accept.

Lifting me lightly,
I abandon the comfort of my shelf.

Turning my pages, he is enamored.
And for once in my life, I am admired.

This was, in the truest of forms.
Love at first sight.

They soften, under your breath.

You

My sharp parts,
Soften, with your touch.

I sip you, silky stone fruit on thy lips.

Pinot Noir

An evening on sunsets time.
Swaying hammock, lying side by side.
Warm days and cool nights.
Humble hearth, a local delight.
The most quality terroir.
Tasted this evening, in pinot noir.
His warm breath sends down a chill.
Down her neck, a lover's thrill.
Running into love, a marathon high.
His strong embrace and dark blue eyes.
Explicit words form little grins.
On wine red lips, a soft crimson.
She searched for no one, to be found on a whim.
Now all she ever wanted, was forever him.

B. K. Sweeting

Tufted Ottoman

Sheer pantyhose, derriere to toes.
Smooth ebony skin highlighted under those.

Sitting on the ottoman that held her secrets.
Vintage gray, tufted velvet.

Fine beauty trifecta, rouge lips and scent.
To the cultured pearls, around her neck.

Gaze brought to vanity, once owned by a lover.
Only mere thoughts now, no need to recover.

Ready, she gracefully makes her way down.
Scintillating, in a silky gown.

Awaiting her presence, where she last placed him on.
Stoic and effervescent, Mr. Perignon.

"It's lovely to have you tonight, Dom."
Little did he know, melon prosciutto would soon join them.

B. K. Sweeting

Illumination

She makes me feel illuminated.
An ethereal, glossy type of sedated.
She simply brightens up my life.
The natural way, unfiltered lights.
She listens and offers cloudless advice.
Luminous girl, this feels so right.
Our chests, beating hot bliss.
We share, an endorphin-laced kiss.
The charming part you cannot resist.
No, you cannot resist, when ecstatic persists.

Bourbon Kiss

Leaf raking sessions, a weekly chore.
Working hard, for that holiday core.
You in a flannel, me in tall boots.
Down home cooking, hearty stews.
Yellow and blood orange, paper lanterns.
Nutty cheese and wine filled decanters.
Bountiful harvest, farmers heart rejoices.
Upstate tractor rides and tall corn mazes.
I fall into you, for a desired frisk.
Holding me tight, planting a bourbon kiss.

B. K. Sweeting

Distance

Ten years old, to ten years there.
Ten years back, but you are not here.
Lake effect snow brought us close.
Now separate lives, flourish on two coasts.

The distance between, of 13 million feet.
I dreamt of you, you dreamt of me.
Mirroring sequence, unknowingly.
Touch felt, only in sleepy memory.

We could be anywhere,
And still to heart, be unfair.
Dwelling love to bestow.
Distant skin, that we cannot let go.

B. K. Sweeting

Dating Labels

She started with Marc.
Though he could not hit the mark.
Lucky to meet Tiffany,
An elegant epiphany.
Louis, a sun god of sorts.
Christian, who blew big red hearts.
Chanel, a living masterpiece.
To Saint, her black and white peace.
Next Thomas, she could never part.
Cashmere care bears and fine plaid art.
He shared ecological passion.
Not always elitist in fashion.
But he was soft, stayed classic.
And felt what she felt.
So, when she thinks of love.
She sports his house check belt.

Merry Mary

Her red sole heels, coming down the hall.
Red and green frames occupy the wall.

Fresh garland, pine and warm hot toddies.
She meets me halfway, to admire my body.

"Thank you, for the eternity rose you sent,
Will you leave at midnight or be the real gift?"

She pulls my long hair, away from my face.
Admittedly says, she will love me always.

Adding, she understands this passion was not a phase.
And that we can now live a life, of boundless holidays.

B. K. Sweeting

Chocolate Croissant

The wrong plus one, influenced a life of solo.
Now evenings of ease, always just so.
Favorite sweaters and homemade cocoa.
Paired tonight, with laminated dough.
Background Sinatra, a warm state of being.
With little dances, ever poetic and freeing.
Setting the tone, for a real deserved bite.
Loving herself, was the new sweet life.

Trust the solitude, sometimes it can bring you back to you.

Solitude

Years of our life we tried, not quite a lifetime.
The end was like a papercut, short but a stinging rough.
An aftershock from quake of heart.
The days that followed, were the hardest part.
Muddled mind, thoughts troubled and hazy.
Initially what felt like, would never leave me.
Agony, had me seeking distractions of friends and family.
Though it was learning to be alone,
That transcendently, built me a healthy home.

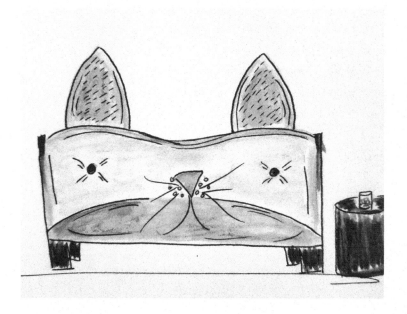

Purr Suede

Saturday frisky.
Kitten on suede couch.
Ice in whisky.
Novel in hand.
Fire going briskly.

Ice

Forced to lie on a slab of ice.
To live out, every shivering slice.
A frozen drama, that was not so nice.
Filled with torment and will to survive.

Sleep paralysis again.
Painful recollection deepens.
Remembering you, tends to hold me back.
Unbarred, but reality lacks.

I could hear my sisters voice,
Screaming to skate hard, but I had no choice.
Sometimes the best of us, must fake a death.
To finally live and take our first breath.

Dance for your life.

Jubilant

Eyes watching, but you are no bore.
There's satisfaction, to explore.
Hop, pop, leap, drop.
Sway hips do not stop.
Feel it, work it, move it more.
Body twisting, out the door.
On the stairs, on the floor.
Feels so good, get so sore.
You like it, they want it.
To work, to the store.
Get loose, flex core.
Heart racing make it soar.

B. K. Sweeting

Scene Stirs

Summer septum seems so far away.
Wearing Vans, to the Penny Arcade.
As young adults, we teased and played.
Beach tag and comparing ear gauge.
Screamo rock and strawberry custard cones.
Holding hands, ferry to Toronto.
Donated to Locks of Love, to cut and dye.
Dramatic bangs always covered one eye.
New York state of mind, with no compromise.
Of mapping out, our artistic lives.
Although the scene was set, I had left.
To pursue new, with a California sunset.

B. K. Sweeting

Visitor

I saw you in my dream again.
Perks of undergoing REM.

Passing out to live a fantasy,
Where we are back together,
Living on the sea.

Bleach

Bleach blonde lock of mine.
Some wear it well, some wear it fine.

Too many bottles, poisoned my mind.
Enduring a life of no reason, nor rhyme.

Original was not what he wanted.
Couldn't keep up, left to be haunted.

By chanting ghosts.
Repeating, "focus on him most."

Questioning myself, where did I go?
Blank walls answer, "only box dyes know."

All this time, I should have been me.
Not masking my needs, frequently.

Abandoned truth, depth and honesty.
For a farse and crumbling dynasty.

Using peroxide as a starter fuel.
To burn our time, that ran too cruel.

B. K. Sweeting

Strangers
Unknown mind, eager to pick.
Craving curves, from lips to hips.

Emotions.
Learning.
Growing.

Unlikeness.
Suspicion.
Betrayals.

Nothing to touch, nothing to find.
Out of sight, out of mind.
Strangers.

Hourglass

It takes two glass bulbs, to form an hourglass.
Only most intimately connected, when the timing is right.

B. K. Sweeting

Ghosts

Ghosts of her heart,
Typed away with darts.
A swiped-right target,
All from the start.
Ample weeks, he was there.
Where is he now? Disdain to bare.
New profile proved; he was not dead.
Just conveniently left, all the words unsaid.

B. K. Sweeting

Starving Artist

Placed a dime-size of oil, on a blank canvas.
My brush befriends crimson red.
Sweeping my brush to the right,
Hastily, swiping left.
…Just like dating.
Desire to paint my love story.
A perfect image remains in my mind.
Though I could never truly, get it just right.

B. K. Sweeting

Spoiler Alert

Companionship, not a project.
That is what canvases are for.

A soft becoming, not sharp.
Enough studs reside on your heels.

Authentic, something whole.
Not crumbs leading, to a fourth of a maybe.

Organic, something to grow.
Not an industrial-chic collection of selfies.

I know, I know.
I have been in that theater too.

Watching my own movie, reel by reel.
I did not want to spoil the end…

But it is a good one,
Do not give up.

B. K. Sweeting

Everything

Feel it.
Talk about it.
Write about it.

Love is not everything.
But the notion that we can again, is.

We Can

You are black, white, tan, freckled.
Mocha, blonde roast and espresso.

You are kind, handsome and funny as hell.
Yeah that guy, plenty of jokes to tell.

I care where you are from, to know you better.
Ancestry and tradition, of ugly sewn sweaters.

We bleed the same, breathe the same air.
Judgement is hard and life is not fair.

But we can be…

We can love who we want and be loved back.
Create a world, where inclusivity does not lack.

To love one another for character and heart.
For richer or poorer, far after the start.

B. K. Sweeting

Appaloosa

On the back of the eldest, domesticated breed.
They rode to the shore, in romantic liberty.

B. K. Sweeting

Heat Dry

Flatware,
In underwear.
A big spoon,
A little spoon.
Cuddle me,
Until I swoon.

B. K. Sweeting

Swash

September visit, every sundown.
Perpetually, where you wash ashore.
Always chasing after a collapsing swell.

I too, was broken when we met.
The waves of you, crashed over me.
Lusting in a sea of desire.

Exhilarating and adventurous.
Quick to learn, your depth is treacherous.
Uprush on the weak, but I know how to swim.

Still longing, for the setting sun.
But the best view, lies in your path.
Do not pull me back in, I have been freed of your wrath.

B. K. Sweeting

I wonder if the sea,
Looks to the moon too,
And thinks of me.

Palm

Plenary, but you have added a new dimension.
Overfilling, my beating organ and expanding my mind.
Feeling the heat, not from the beating sun.
But your eyes, like pretty little laser pointers.

Dancing and flailing arms, around the desert palm.
Hair flowing, air dry and running breathless.
You bring me to a stop, pulling my head back.
Caressing my lips, with your lips.
Delectable, sweet and salty mix.

B. K. Sweeting

Strawberry Ice Cream

Fresh cut lawn and pink peonies.

Picnic blanket, under the apple trees.

Removing my strap, my heart starts to swell.

Touching skin, you tease so well.

Stomach tight, feeling a drop.

You chose me, please never stop.

I surprise you with a treat,

Your eyes start to beam.

You then take a lick –

Of my strawberry ice cream.

Among the Sunflowers

A beautifully lit, Summer day.
Exploring a row of tall sunflowers.
Ahead, was the first boy he told his secrets to.
Who was also, the first man to touch his soul.
A high skin fade and hard comb over.
Poised confidence and defined back muscles.
Letting a light laugh out, oh those tan cargo shorts,
The ones he could never quite part from.
Nearing end of path, he drops to a knee.
From his pocket, he exposes a small box.
His equal before him, halts upon the silence.
Turning around, to face his absolute best friend.
An unexpected sight to see.
Followed by a pause, causing a tear.

Marram

Auburn hair twisted into a fishtail braid.
Wispy pieces framed her porcelain face.

A band of freckles marched across her nose.
A coo in the distance, to which she rose.

Seeking sound along the cliff, that welcomed the sea below.
Watching her step, tall grasses to and fro.

A winsome creature perched tableside, wondering how this was so?
This was their spot; Weston built that 7 years ago.

A dove out this way, was out of the ordinary.
Perhaps a seagull or a glass blown canary.

Content thoughts, tickled her mind,
Observing his work, where he truly shined.

Her white feathered friend gently flew away.
"I miss you Wes, forever and a day."

B. K. Sweeting

Bae is Bay

Gifts for no reason,
Like lovers should.
A bouquet of salt,
Cypress and driftwood.

A soft foghorn,
Wailing in the distance,
Seagulls murmur,
A melodic consistence.

The coast always granting,
An enchanting breeze.
Knowingly, the bay,
Rocks me into tranquility.

B. K. Sweeting

Brittany

The hot gusty Summer, of 1944.
Soldiers, one million troops from shore to shore.

Starting at Brittany, the northern tip.
France in need, to be freed of considerable debt.

A debt of economical ruin, lives and land taken over.
Battle success of Brest, where he also saved his lover.

B. K. Sweeting

Evermore at The Moor

"Par la mer", she whispered in his ear.
Where they first locked eyes on the coast.
Reunited to view, waves on waves.
Sapphire, royals and ultramarine.
A reminiscent flutter, like bubbly in their chest.
The water ahead sparkled, like the diamond he revealed.
Held steadfast, through a world war.
Resting his forehead against hers.
He whispered back, "by the sea, marry me."
Sliding the rock on her dainty, 94-year-old finger.
An incandescent deep held lifelong love.

Tidal Devotion

She dove right into,
Swirls of deep Prussian, that grew.
Entangled within, the velvet hues.
Swimming against current, is not easy to do.
He was the one, tender and true.
Not the strain and pain of heavy-weighted blues.
She let the waves of his praise, submerge her.
In sets, then altogether.
They anchored, through all types of weather.
A give and take, that could never be better.

Acknowledgements

For those who contributed their eyes and ears limitlessly
on this book: Thank you to my Wonder Woman of a Mom,
my little brother, Robert and his cat, Tommy, Mary
and Richard. You helped make this happen, I love you.

For those that were taken far too soon, though I know
you're watching from above: My big brother, Christopher.
My best friend, Alex. And my second mama, Sue.

And thank you to you, the reader.
For taking the time to read the words, see the illustrations
and feel the feels. You are wonderful and you are loved.

If you or someone you know is suffering,
please seek the following:

Treatment Hotline: 1-800-662-4357
Suicide Hotline: 1-800-273-8255
Alcoholics Anonymous: Aa.org
♥